INSTEAD SAY THIS
FOR PARENTS OF INFANTS

By Kishon M. Whittier, PsyD, LP

Instead Say This...
For Parents of Infants
Copyright © 2020 by Kishon M. Whittier
ISBN: 9781087887791

Dedicated to the Infant Team and Parent Child Program of St. David's Center for Child & Family Development

This book may be helpful for parents who would like some guidance in sorting out both their own and their infant's feelings. Talking to our baby about what he or she may be experiencing allows us to organize our own feelings and understand our infant's behaviors and emotions. When we have a better understanding of their behaviors and emotions, we can respond in a more supportive way.

It is surprisingly helpful to say things in a more specific and accurate way - a way that blames neither us nor our child. When we say things differently, we are able to feel differently.

The format of this book is as follows: The page on the left is something we might say to our infant. The page on the right offers an alternative that better supports our infant's social and emotional development.

I don't know why you're crying! I fed you and changed you.

Instead say…

Right now you just need to cry and need me to hold you. Don't worry. I'm here. I've got you.

I know you're tired, you just need to fall asleep.

Instead say…

It's hard to regulate your body- this is all so new to you. I am here to be with you and help you regulate.

I don't like you.

Instead say…

This is not what I expected, but I will hang in there with you and we'll figure it out.

You are being so naughty!

Instead say…

It seems like you are manipulating me, but I know that as an infant that is not developmentally possible.

I just need a minute to myself!

Instead say…

Right now, I am feeling too frustrated/angry to be with you. I will come back in five minutes after I try to calm down. (I will put you in a safe place like your crib so I know you will be safe).

Why do you always calm down with him/her and not with me? I guess you like them better.

Instead say…

I'm glad you feel calmer with him/her *and* it hurts my feelings that you don't calm down with me as easily. I know that you aren't doing this intentionally though. You are an infant and not capable of that.

Why don't you drink more?

Instead say…

I will do what I can to make you comfortable and not distracted while feeding you and I will trust when you are finished, even if the bottle is not empty.

I guess I don't have the right equipment to be good at breastfeeding you. Something is wrong with me.

Instead say…

My body is good enough and works just fine. We have to figure out how to work together. Let's keep trying, but right now, I need a break.

I am not good enough.

Instead say…

This is hard and I am enough.

Why can't you let me get some sleep?!

Instead, say...

I am getting too tired and run down. I need to ask for support and help. I don't have to do this alone.

I am so tired of changing your diaper! Stop pooping!

Instead say...

Wow, this is redundant and tiring. However, I am glad your bowels are in working order.

You really embarrassed me in that store!

Instead say…

I am feeling very embarrassed and worried what people think of me. Maybe that wasn't the best time to take you to the store or it was just a hard situation for us.

You were supposed to fall asleep in the car!

Instead say…

I was hoping you'd fall asleep in the car and I know it's different from what you are used to. We will figure it out when we get there.

Don't look at me like that!

Instead say...

You are able to make so many new facial expressions and I know they are not all intentional- you still don't have full control of your muscles!

Shouldn't you be sleeping through the night by now?

Instead say…

I really need more sleep and I had hoped you'd be sleeping through the night by now. I know all babies are different and I am not doing anything wrong.

Why do I have to do everything for you?

Instead say…

It's hard doing everything for you. I know it is necessary and I know it won't always be like this.

I get so bored playing with you!

Instead say...

I am not used to this pace. I will try to slow myself down and play on the floor with you, doing what you do and smiling a lot.

You are such a difficult baby.

Instead say...

This is much harder than I thought it would be.
I am here with you.

You are going to be so stubborn!

Instead say…

I am noticing your personality come out little by little, but it is too soon to label you as anything yet.

You are so weird!

Instead say…

You do some silly/weird things!

You're going to be such a...

Instead say...

I am interested to see who you become.

You like your dada/mama better.

Instead say...

You seem more content with your dada/mama right now. I won't take it personally and will keep coming back to you.

You are such a picky eater.

Instead say...

I know that it takes many tastes of a food before a baby gets used to the flavor, so I will keep introducing you to this food because I know it is good for you.

I am not going to feed you this! It tastes terrible.

Instead say...

Even though my taste buds tell me this is gross, I know you experience tastes differently. Since I know this is a healthy food for you, I will continue to feed it to you.

You are exactly like your dad/mom.

Instead say…

While I see similarities between you and your dad/mom,
I know that you are your own individual person.

There's no point in reading to you. You're just a baby and I feel weird doing it.

Instead say…

Even though it feels a little strange to be reading to you,
I will trust the research that says reading to you helps
you develop language.

You get sick all the time. What am I doing wrong?

Instead say...

I know I am doing my best to keep you healthy. There are just a lot of germs out there that your little body is working hard to develop immunity against.

You are the smartest baby ever!

Instead say...

I am so proud of your development and feel so lucky to have a healthy and happy baby.

How come you aren't crawling yet?

Instead say…

It's okay that you are not crawling yet. I know you are developing at your own pace.

You seriously can't be hungry again.

Instead say…

Although you ate only a little while ago, you are showing me signs that you are hungry.

I know you hate tummy time, but everyone keeps saying how important it is. I hate to see you cry.

Instead say…

Let's compromise. Because I know tummy time builds important muscles for you, let's try it for a little bit each day until your muscles get strong enough to do it a little longer.

I just gave you a bath and now you have a blowout. I swear you are doing this on purpose.

Instead say…

Wow! What are the chances? Just had a bath…now a blowout! Pretty good I guess since you poop 10-12 times per day. When you gotta go, you gotta go, I guess.

I can't do this.

Instead say...

I will do this and I will get through this. And it's okay to ask for help.

I wish everybody would stop telling me to enjoy my time with you because it goes so fast. These are the longest days of my life!

Instead say...

I am doing the best I can and I am enjoying moments with you.

I can't take you to the doctor again. They will think I am an anxious new dad/mom!

Instead say...

I can and will take you to the doctor as often as I feel necessary. I am your dad/mom and I am going to do what I believe is important regardless of what they may think of me. I have parental instincts.

I am so scared of something harmful happening to you. Why can't I get these worries out of my head?

Instead say…

I know my parental instincts are thinking of all these scenarios as a way to help keep you safe. As frustrating as it is, I will just notice when they come and then let them go as I remind myself you are safe right now.

You are so demanding!

Instead say…

Thanks for being so persistent in letting me know you need me.

Why can't you just calm down by yourself?!

Instead say…

As you continue to develop, you will be more able to regulate your emotions on your own. Right now, you are not equipped to do that at all. I will be your co-regulator. I know just me holding you and us being together is what you need in order to organize and regulate your emotions.

I don't get why you are crying right now. I have tried everything to get you to stop!

Instead say...

You don't need a reason for crying. I am not doing anything wrong and there is not anything for me to figure out to help you stop crying.

You are so loud!!!

Instead say…

I am going to put these ear plugs in so that I can tolerate the sound of your cry a little better. What a set of lungs you have!

You are not what I thought you would look like. You don't even look like my child!

Instead say...

Although you do not look how I had imagined, I know you are mine and how you look will change many times as you get older.

Your eyes are going crossed sometimes, so you probably are going to have eye problems.

Instead say…

Your eye muscles are still developing and getting stronger. Even though your eyes go crossed, that doesn't mean they will always do that or that you will have eye problems.

I need more space! I feel like you are on me constantly!

Instead say…

While I know it's important that you are held often, I am still my own person and it's okay if I take a break from holding you.

I don't feel connected to you and I didn't feel that instant bond or love when you were born. What is wrong with me?!

Instead say…

While some people may feel a bond right away, it is also normal to develop our connection and love over time. After all, we did just meet. I trust that we will become bonded as we spend more time together.

What have I gotten myself into?

Instead say...

We are in this together, for the long haul. Let's take it day by day and accept help from people we trust. I will take care of myself and I will take care of you.

www.ingramcontent.com/pod-product-compliance
Lightning Source LLC
Chambersburg PA
CBHW060501010526
44118CB00018B/2492